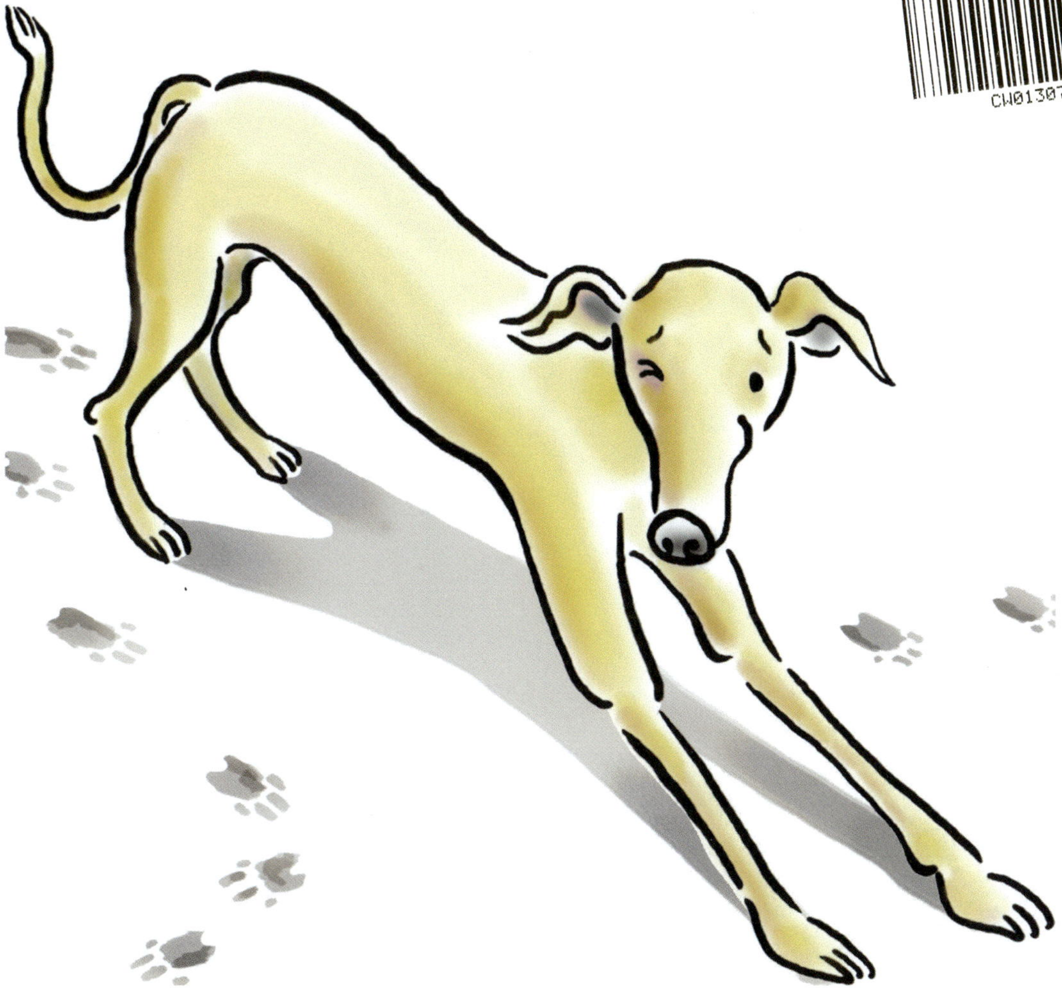

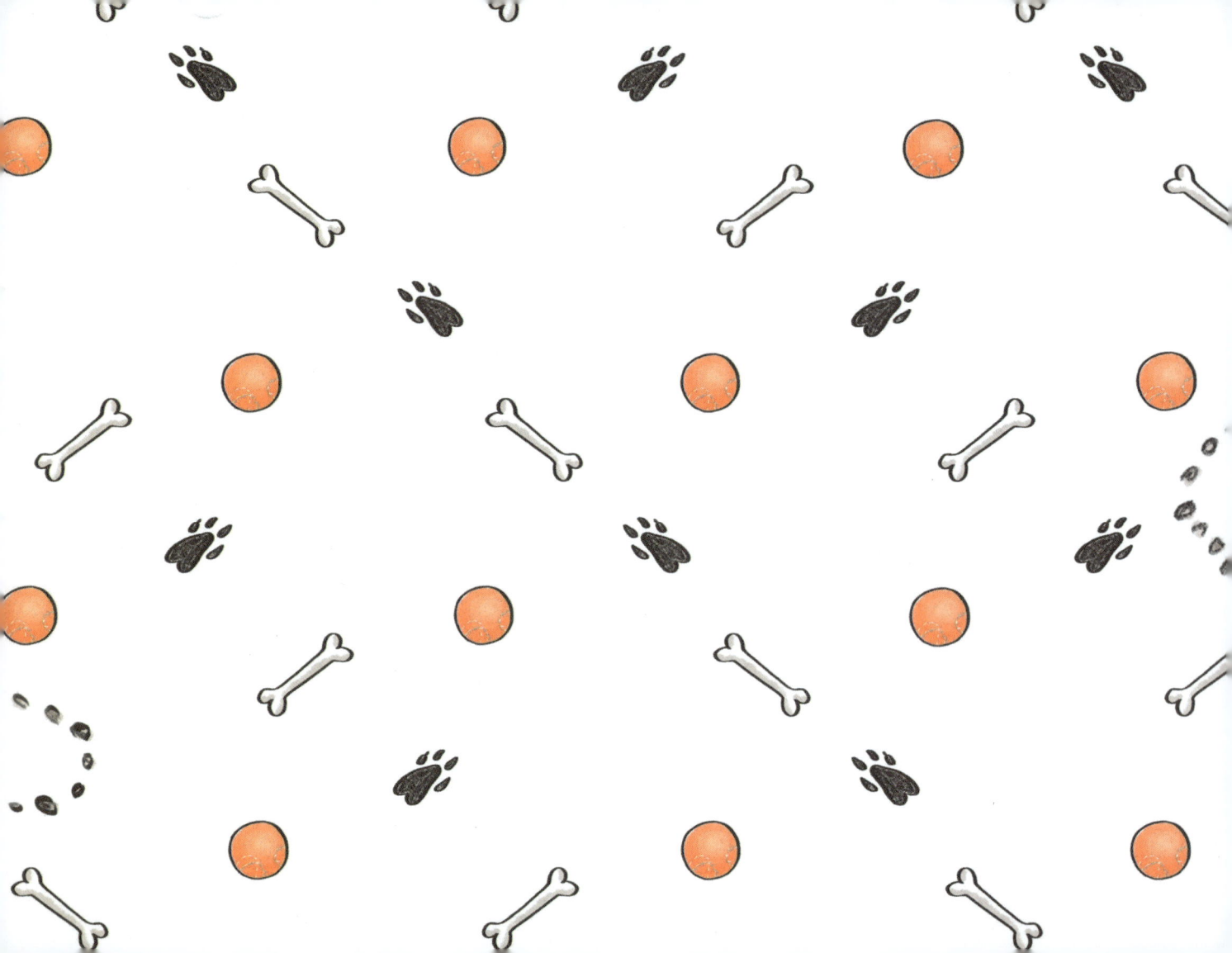

Dogblog: The Diary of Custard-Dog
The First Year
By Jacqui Blore

For Alice love Jacqui x Christmas 2018.

First published in 2018

Copyright © 2018

The rights of the author and illustrator have been asserted in accordance with Sections 77 and 78 of the Copyright Designs and Patents Act, 1988.

All rights reserved.

No part of this book may be reproduced (including photocopying or storing in any medium by electronic means and whether or not transiently or incidentally to some other use of this publication) without the written permission of the copyright holder except in accordance with the provisions of the Copyright, design and patents Act 1988. This book is a work of fiction.

ISBN-13: 978-1790709595

TEAMAUTHOR UK
Publishing with you

Dedication

For my Family

I am a long, tall, narrow dog with a coat of yellow velvet. My name is Custard and, at only a few weeks old, I was dumped at a local veterinary surgery and left for dead. The lovely people at the vet's saved my life and nursed me back to health until I was well enough to go and live at an RSPCA shelter. I had only been at the centre for a short time before a new human came to visit me. Unbeknownst to me at the time, this was to be my own human and I would go and live with her in what became my forever home.

Although it was great to have somewhere permanent to live and get regular food and cuddles, I soon learned that humans have all sorts of illogical rules and regulations, most of which I decided, very early on, to ignore completely. Yes, I am utterly wicked, but I am equally utterly adorable.

I just am; it's indisputable.

My human also has another dog, Calvie, who I love immensely but he is a bit of a goody-two-shoes and always does as he's told. There is also a cat, Mimi; the least said about her the better. You should also know that my human has a niece called Emily and a nephew called Mikey; two of my favourite humans.

From day one I decided to keep a diary of my mischief and misdemeanours:

Friday

I've arrived at my new home - hurray! Oh. It seems I'm not meant to piddle on the carpet here...

Saturday

I've played and played all day with Calvie - he is such a softie and lets me win every game of tug-o-war.

Wednesday

I met some friends of my human today, all of whom had dogs. Cal is already great friends with them so I decided to join in but got my ear bitten! Nooooo! I cried and cried and my human took me to the vet where they had to bandage my head. I felt really stupid with a turban-like thing around my head so, as soon as my human had gone to sleep, I ripped it off and opened up the wound again. Not a good idea, I know, but I did manage to get blood everywhere and got a load more attention when my human woke up and put a smaller, better-looking bandage on my head.

Thursday

I do feel better today and, to prove it, I jumped up and bit my human's bottom as I followed her downstairs...

WELCOME HOME

Friday

Wow! Cal and I had an absolutely mad play in the house today and made a huge mess - so satisfying!

Saturday

Ah, bliss! Last night I discovered that it is warmer under the duvet than on top of it. Best night's sleep ever.

Monday

Just for fun I pulled my human's pyjama trousers out from the bed where she'd neatly folded them and bit a huge hole in the bottom.

Tuesday

I tried so hard to wake my human this morning because I needed to go out; firstly I whined softly but she turned over and went back to sleep; then I barked a little bit but she shoved her head under the pillow and went back to sleep; I started pawing at her but she just pulled the covers over her head and went back to sleep; somehow I managed to get my paw under the pillow and scratched the inside of her nose. It hurt like crazy and bled quite a lot but she just shoved a tissue up her nose and went back to sleep. I gave up and had a massive poo in the kitchen. It stank but at least I managed to do it in the cat litter tray . . .

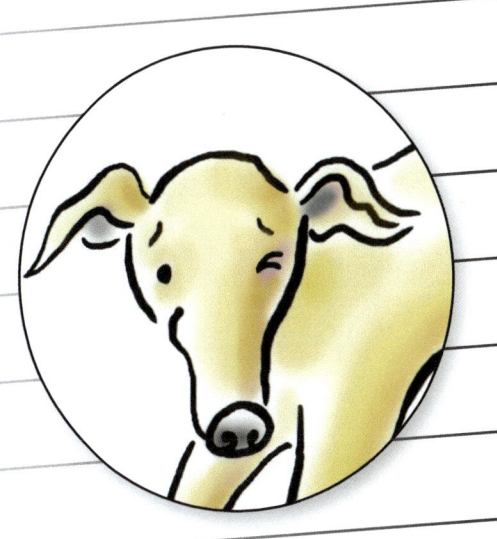

Wednesday

Dear fellow dogs,

I have discovered a lovely new game for you all to play:

1. Jump up onto your human's bed at the headboard end.
2. Shuffle your way under the duvet.
3. Rapidly tunnel your way down to the bottom of the bed.
4. Jump down onto the floor.
5. Scamper back to the top end of the bed and repeat.
6. Repeat.
7. Repeat.
8. Repeat.
9. Repeat.
10. Repeat.

Hope you enjoy the game.

Love, Custard xx

PS *Enhance your enjoyment by playing the game at 3am.*

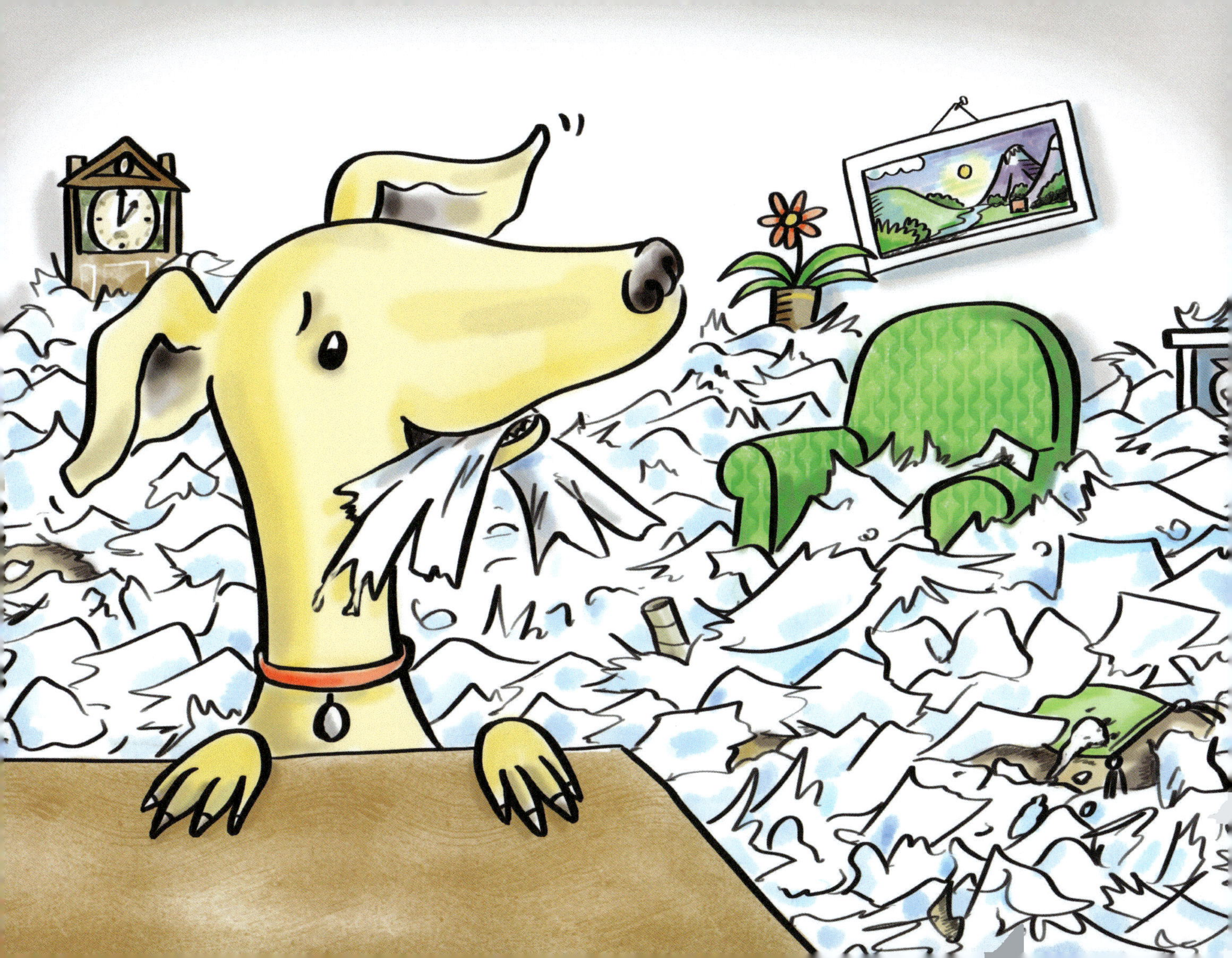

Thursday

I've just discovered that an average-sized kitchen roll, when shredded and chewed, can fill the floor space of an entire room - who knew?!

Friday

For sale - one bedside cabinet, corners only slightly chewed. Hahahaha!

Monday

Oh dear! My human came home from work at lunchtime to discover that I am now tall enough to reach up to the shelf where my antibiotics are. I scoffed a whole week's worth in one go and had to go to the vet and have the most vile charcoal 'treatment'. Not doing that again - yuck!

Tuesday

Snow - not going out in that!

Wednesday

Of course I have no idea how the watering can got in her bed. Why does she ask me these things . . .?

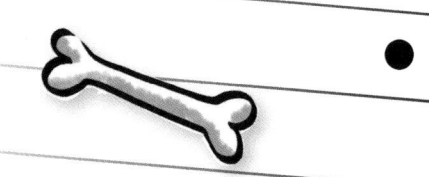

Thursday

Naughty things I did today whilst my human was out:

1. Wee in the hall.
2. Poo in the kitchen.
3. Chewed Emily's Kermit toy.
4. Ate a big chunk of rug.
5. Pulled some books down off a shelf in the bedroom, ripped off the covers and chewed the corners.
6. Chewed a bit of the bookshelf.
7. Carried all my bedding downstairs and left it behind the door so that my human really struggled to get the door open.
8. Destroyed a mystery object made of hard grey plastic - my human still hasn't been able to work out what it is . . .

Life is so much fun!

Friday

I was so exhausted after yesterday's escapades that I was fairly well-behaved today - only a couple of minor infringements to keep my human on the ball:

I chewed a lot more of the bookcase in the bedroom - yummy!

My human always lets us out into the garden first thing in the morning (usually after I've jumped on her head a bit to wake her up - she doesn't need me to do this as she has an alarm clock but I like to do it anyway, just before the alarm goes off. Or, in today's case, at 6.30 am, a good hour before the alarm. Such fun!). Anyway, this morning my human didn't notice that I sneaked back in the house with a big stick from the garden and hid it under her bed. When she was out at work, Calvie and I played and played and played with the stick leaving squillions of shredded bits of stick and mud all over the bedroom - utter carnage! Hilarious!

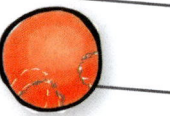

Saturday

Not much opportunity for shenanigans as my human has been in all day but I had fun first thing when I only pretended to have a poo outside and then did it in the kitchen whilst my human was in the shower.
I also instigated a boisterous, noisy play-fight with Calvie when she was watching the rugby.

My human vacuumed upstairs earlier and, when we came back from our walk, I sneaked in with a muddy tennis ball from the garden and rolled it all over the bedroom carpet.

So, all in all, I've not been too naughty today but there is still time. There's always time.

Sunday

Just to lull my human into a false sense of security I have been as good as gold today. Oh, apart from the trampolining on the bed when my human had an afternoon nap. Apparently she had to have an afternoon nap because I woke her up at 6 am. Of course I did, I wanted to play!

Monday

I am the naughtiest puppy EVER today!! So pleased with that. Other than hiding my human's slippers occasionally, I have never shown any interest in eating footwear. Until today. Leather is sooooo chewy and lovely - yum! How was I to know that they were expensive, new boots she had for her birthday? (TBH it wouldn't have made any difference if I had known . . .) And then, having developed a taste for leather, I had a good old chew of her purse (and a couple of bank cards and a £10 note - not so nice). Because I didn't like being shouted at, I piddled on the floor right in front of her. That'll teach her!

What a fun day!

Tuesday

Yes, I freely admit to eating loads of stuff I shouldn't but, all the same, I can't really be blamed for having diarrhoea, can I? And the fact that I splattered a great load of it out in the middle of a zebra-crossing on a very busy street in town cannot be helped. Or can it?! *Hahaha!*

Wednesday

Yessssss! Nailed it like a boss!!

For a while now, I have been hatching the cunningest of cunning plans, and today I carried it out with spectacular aplomb.

My human made her lunch (paté on toast) and no sooner had she sat down at the table to eat it than I started scratching and whining pathetically at the back door to indicate that I needed to go out. Knowing my track record with 'accidents' in the house (tee hee!) she got up immediately to let me out. As she got to the back door, I shot back, lickety-split, into the kitchen, grabbed her lunch off the table, wolfed it down in one go and disappeared upstairs. It was the most perfect manoeuvre, even if I say so myself. Absolute genius!

Yessssss! Nailed it like a boss!!

Thursday

I like to keep my human guessing so have been really well-behaved today (apart from destroying one of the solar lights in the garden and eating a big hole in a pair of my human's trousers - well I am only a puppy, what do you expect?!).

Big day tomorrow though - apparently I am going to spend the day at the vet's. I love it there as it was where I was taken when I was abandoned. They saved my life and made me well so that my human could adopt me.

Every time I go there, they all come out to make a big fuss of me and treat my like a celebrity, which is only to be expected if I'm honest. I am rather wonderful.

So, I'm not sure why I'm going to the vet's; my human mentioned something about "balls" - I don't really ever listen to her properly but presumably I'm going there to play all day . . .

Friday

Oh. My. Dog. I have been unmanned, emasculated, castrated - they've taken my bollocks when I wasn't looking! I am bereft. Life will never be the same again. No more Custard genes to spread round the world. It is a bad, sad day.

Saturday

Ate one more solar light from the garden and piddled in the house three times. Still cross about my testicles.

Sunday

Crept into the bathroom this morning as my human was cleaning her teeth. Stuck my cold, wet nose up her bottom - ha! She jumped so much that she banged her head on the shower door. That'll teach her for having me 'done'. Still sore.

Monday

There was a piece about me in the local newspaper today from the vet's who saved me. They noted that I had kept my name. How stupid; I would rather have kept my bollocks.

Thursday

I tried SO hard to be good yesterday, I really, really did, but some things are impossible to resist; my human brought a couple of trays of seedlings out of the greenhouse to plant out. Whilst she was faffing in the garage I ate one tray of seedlings and did a big sloppy poo on the other. Couldn't help it. Will she never learn?! (I hope not as I might not have so much fun if she does - ha!)

Saturday

One of you miserable so-and-so's suggested to my human that she smear mustard on furniture so that I won't eat it. My favourite most edible bookshelf now tastes absolutely revolting - thanks a lot!

Mind you, it didn't stop me - I ate lots more of it just so I could be sick all over the living-room carpet.

Monday

Toothpaste?!! Blearrggh! How can you humans stand the taste of it?! I stole a tube of it from the bathroom this morning and disliked it so much that I smeared it all over the landing carpet. Even managed to get some on the cat.

Vile stuff.

Wednesday

It's not my fault, it really isn't!
In her haste to feed us before going out to a rehearsal this evening, my human didn't close the door to the food cupboard properly . . .

I ate and ate and ate and ate and ate - probably about 6 tons of dog biscuits (mostly Calvie's - I'm not daft!) - until I was sick everywhere. Oh, and then my bottom exploded, too. Messy. Very messy. And smelly.
I'd do it again though . . .

Sunday

My human went to stay with friends this weekend and Calvie and I stayed with some different friends. I was the perfect house-guest . . .

Just one or two very minor indiscretions - hardly worth mentioning really - such as a couple of poos in their bedroom, stealing a load of cutlery from their dishwasher and stashing the items away in hard-to-find-places so that

I could enjoy gnawing on them later, at my leisure. And of course I have absolutely no idea whatsoever where the packet of butter went . . .

Even though I had a lovely holiday, I was a bit cross that my human had gone away without us so I did a big poo in the garage just now, as she was mowing the lawn - she hasn't found it yet . . .

Monday

I don't understand my human. I thought she would be grateful. She hates her alarm clock, swears at it and throws it across the room every morning. And yet she seems cross that I've chewed it to bits . . .

Tuesday

My human says she is going to find the people who abandoned me and hand me back.

She's very upset with me but I was only having some fun whilst she was asleep - this is always possible because she sleeps so soundly and nothing wakes her up; it's brilliant!

My human hides the cat food on the high shelf of a bookcase so that I can't reach it. It foxed me for a long time but I sussed it last night - I pulled the bookcase over. This meant that not only could I eat all the cat food but I could nibble the edges of lots of her books as well - yum!

And of course, because I had gorged on so much nice, rich cat food, I then had to poo all over the kitchen floor.

My human slept through it all so just imagine her surprise when she woke up this morning - ha!

Wednesday

Today has been epic - one of the best days of my life so far! My human has a 'flu-like' bug and has been in bed all day, practically dead to the world. First of all I persuaded Calvie to join me in a game I call "hoppity jump" on my human's bed - we did it for ages before turning it into the longest dog-wrestling match in the world, ever.

Then, when that didn't disturb her enough, we had a bark-off - Cal and I stand nose to nose and just bark and bark and bark. Not for any reason, just because we can.

My human complained so we calmed down for a while. I waited until she was fast asleep again and then I started chewing a corner of my bed (it's an old duvet) until loads and loads of feathers came out. Cal and I chased these all round the house - they got everywhere. It was magic!

Then we played stair races - running up and down the stairs as quickly and as loudly as possible - the cat even joined in as well.

Then I ate a significant amount of my favourite bookcase after which I needed to go out so pawed and scratched at my human until she got up.

Now that my human is up and about, Cal and I have gone to sleep - we're exhausted!

(Mind you, she'll probably go back to bed in a bit, so I'll have to think of some more fun games - can't wait!)

Thursday

You see, I'm not all bad. My human really isn't very well at all and she was all shivery and cold when she went to bed last night so I snuck in beside her and snuggled up to her with my soft, velvet coat and kept her warm all night. I wasn't even tempted to get out and eat my favourite bookcase or go downstairs and wee in the kitchen - well, not much anyway . . .

Friday

I felt sorry for my human last night as she was still quite ill so I cuddled up to her and kept her warm again (she didn't realise it, but she spent most of the night with one of my back feet up her nose - ha!) I didn't prowl around causing mayhem, I stayed put with her all night long. Aren't I good?

Good is boring though, don't you think? And naturally, I couldn't keep it up for long; when my human went for a shower this morning, I realised she had left the living room door open - whoop whoop! The bowl of potpourri was soon overturned and scattered all over the sofa and floor. I did eat some but it was vile. I pulled all the cushions and throws off the sofa and chairs and had a bit of a fight with them - just a couple of tears here and there, not a huge amount of damage. In hindsight, I could've done better.

When my human came downstairs she chased me out into the garden and shut the door on me. Yes, she actually shut me out! I couldn't believe it either. So I completely obliterated the outside edge of the cat flap in retaliation and she couldn't hear me doing this because she was vacuuming up the mess I had made in the living room. She eventually let me back in but I was still cross that she had shut me out so I stole a croissant that was warming under the grill. I burnt my nose a little bit but boy was it worth it! Croissants are delicious!

Friday - Part 2

Damn! My human has just found my stash of kitchen knives in the garden! (I steal these from the sink - serves her right for not washing up immediately after a meal!)

Sunday

Yesterday was awesome! My human was away all day playing in an orchestra in Welshpool and left Calvie and me with friends. These humans live with Calvie's mum and brother as well as another lurcher like me, and they live in acres of glorious countryside so we spent all day running and running and chasing and chasing and playing and playing. I was having such an amazing time that I completely forgot to be naughty!

But, do you know what is really bizarre? Last time I stayed with these humans, the butter disappeared from the dish on the kitchen island - and it did this time as well! How weird is that?!

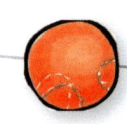

Monday

My human was working from home today so opportunities for shenanigans were limited, unfortunately.

This morning was exciting though; I've been having Messenger chats with a canine fan, Bailey, and he and his human came to visit. Well, we roared around and played and barked and did loads of dog stuff until Bailey's human put him on the lead to calm him down. I then spent the rest of the visit tormenting him because I knew he couldn't get free to teach me a lesson - hahaha! He was lovely though and I hope he visits again.

Finally my human went out this evening, just for 10 minutes or so to collect some flyers. Plenty of time to create havoc and make up for lost time. You might know that she has to plaster her finger every day (she had some kind of accident and it has to be stretched and plastered twice a day) so has loads and loads of plaster of Paris bandages. They were put well out of my reach but I keep growing. This evening I discovered that I could reach the bandages so I pulled them all down, chewed off the wrappers, ate some of the bandages (blearrggh!) and spread all the chalky, dry powder stuff off the bandages all over the kitchen. I then chased Calvie around through all the powder and off upstairs so that we got white powdery footprints all over the house! It took my human such a long time to clear it all up. Fantastic fun!

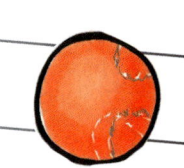

Tuesday

Not sure what all the fuss is about, it wasn't a particularly nice rug anyway. I just wanted to see if it tasted better than it looked . . .

Tuesday - Part 2

I am SOOOOOOOO bad. My human made up the bed in the spare room just now for her guests coming to stay tomorrow. The door to this room is usually closed and I'm not allowed in ever since I had a rather nasty tummy explosion in there when I was small . . .

Anyway, my human had just finished making the bed, she came out onto the landing to get some towels out of the laundry cupboard and, quick as lightning, I dashed into the room and did a wee on the bed - cool or what?

Wednesday

First of all, I think I should make it clear that it was not my fault I was naughty today - Cal and I were abandoned, utterly abandoned, for 3 whole hours whilst my human went out and had fun. Ok yes, she did arrange for a friend to come and let us out and have a run round the garden half-way through her absence but that's not the point; she wasn't here.

So I managed to get her cycle helmet down off the peg in the hall and chewed it to bits - I didn't eat much of it but managed to leave a huge trail of mangled carnage all over the hall and kitchen.

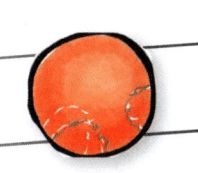

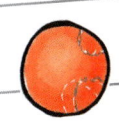

Then I had a poo on the rug in the hall, 2 widdles in the kitchen, and threw up in my human's bedroom. I think she got off lightly, considering . . .

Thursday

I know you won't believe it but I have been exceptionally good today - honest. We've spent nearly all day with my human's niece and nephew, roaring around chasing sticks, catching balls, playing football, and practising kangaroo jumps. I'm exhausted and need to recharge my batteries before instigating any more mischief. I'll be back!

Friday

Yesterday's good behaviour could not last; I knew it, you all knew it and, deep down, my human knew it too.

Today I stole one of my human's slippers, one of my human's brother's slippers, and one of my human's sister-in-law's slippers, and then I hid them all in different places. It was such fun watching them hopping round trying to find them.

But, my pièce de resistance today, well, even I feel I have excelled myself: Do any of you remember a while back that I had eaten a mystery object of grey plastic? My human and her guests only discovered today (when it was too late - ha!) that the grey plastic had been the cover of the junction box in the hall where my human's telephone and internet come into the house.

Whilst they were all out this evening, I decided it was as good a time as any to chew up all the wires and fittings in the junction box. After all, telephones and the internet are of no use to me whatsoever so what do I care . . .?

PS I am so very cross that my human's brother was able to rewire the junction box and fix the phone line and now the humans are all sitting round using their mobile devices instead of paying attention to me!

Monday

Humans can be very ungrateful at times; I spent ages yesterday tearing apart a full box of tissues into tiny scraps to make a magical snow scene in the hall and kitchen for my human. All that effort and she didn't even thank me . . .

Tuesday

I had another go at a snowscape again today but with lovely, brightly coloured paper from Easter present gift bags. I think I created a remarkably beautiful floral effect through the hall, up the stairs, across the landing and into my human's bed but she STILL didn't appreciated my efforts - I just don't understand it . . .

Wednesday

Blimey, my human can be a right pain! After I'd chewed the telephone junction box and cut off her phone line, her brother mended it and she made a rather pathetic makeshift cover out of cardboard to try to stop me doing it again. Ha! I destroyed that within seconds of her leaving the house (but didn't quite manage to get to the wires this time - must try harder). Then my human made another cover out of chicken wire but I destroyed that, too (again, I didn't quite manage to eat through the wires - perhaps I'm losing my touch?).

Today my human has made a wooden box covered in gaffer tape to prevent me from eating the wires, but I just laughed as she was doing it because wood and gaffer tape are two of my favourite things to eat - I can't believe she didn't realise that! Humans can be so stupid at times.

But you'll never guess what she did next; she smeared mustard over the whole thing! It's so horrible that it nearly made me sick! My human is so mean - where's the fun in that?!

Thursday

I was delighted to receive a letter from the Plaid Cymru candidate today - it tasted lovely!

Friday

Well, that's a great morning's work; good-sized nibble marks on every piece of bedroom furniture.

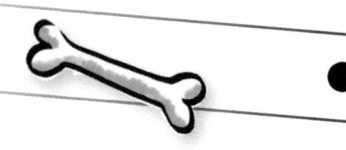

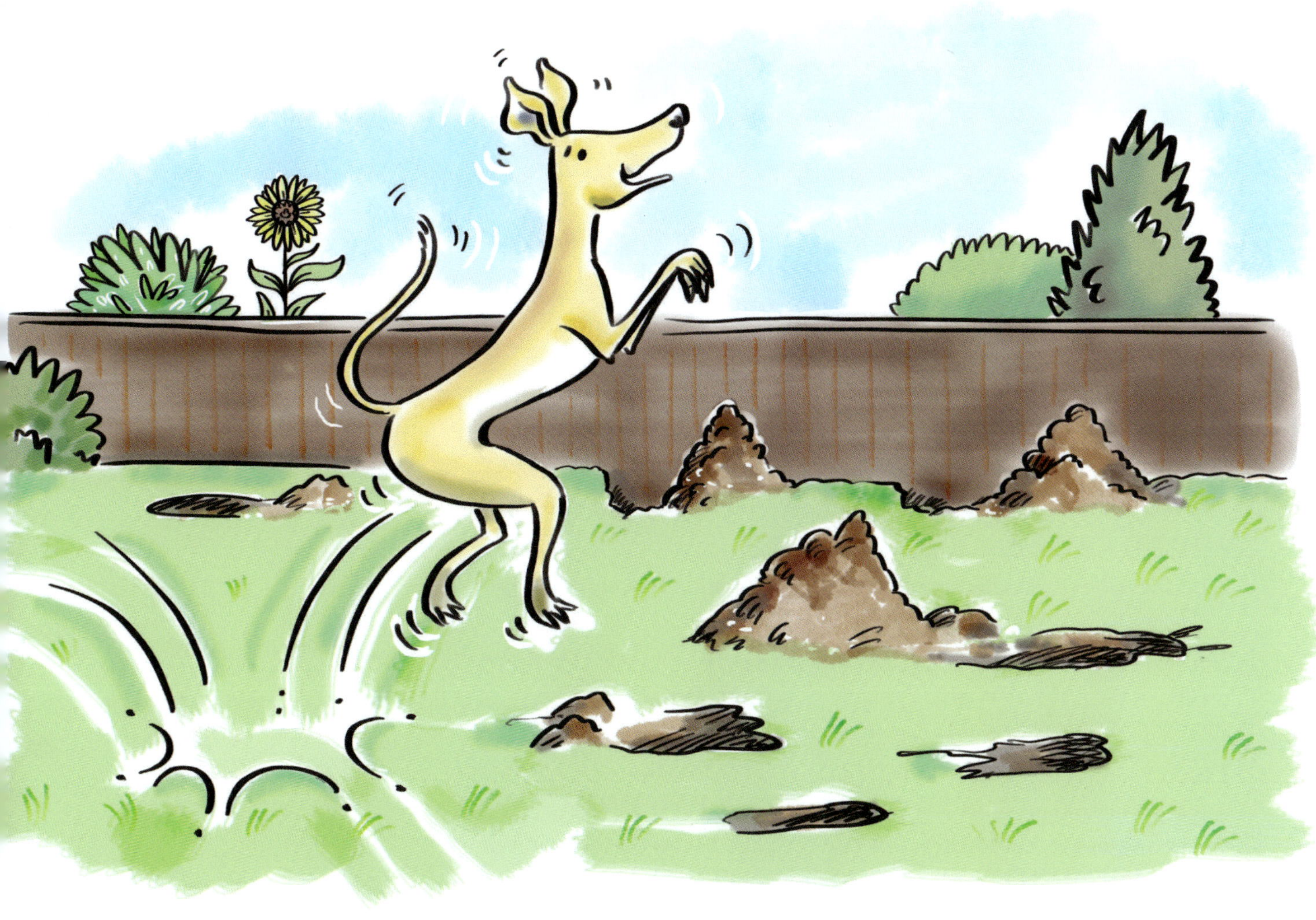

Saturday

This morning, when I was out in the garden practicing my kangaroo jumps, I discovered that I could dig holes in the lawn - yay!

Monday

When she dashed off to work this morning, my human didn't close the wardrobe door properly and left the arm of a blouse sticking out, so I ate it!

Tuesday

My human only popped out for a bit to go and visit her parents but, having been so good over the past few days (ha!), I took full advantage of her absence:

1. I've not 'messed' in the house for ages so I did a poo in the kitchen and a wee in the hall.
2. I ate the nose off my human's big cuddly toy panda that she's had since she was tiny and pulled out some of his stuffing.
3. I destroyed the brand new dog bed my human bought this afternoon (to replace the one I had widdled on just once too often. Calvie uses it more than I do which is why I wee on it, tee hee!).
4. I found a clothes-peg and destroyed most of it. My human can't find the metal spring bit and is worried I've eaten it and that it will cut me inside. (Just between us, it's buried in my bed upstairs. I have no intention of eating it but just wanted to scare her. Don't tell.)

5. When she came home and was busy clearing up my mess, I ran outside and ate all her sunflower seedlings.

My human asked me when I was going to start being good. I told her I was working towards the 1st of Never...

Thursday

My human thinks there is definitely improvement in my behaviour today - not a single 'accident' in the house when she was at work.
But I did upend the laundry basket and ate a pair of knickers and a sock.
Oh, and I ate the handle of the laundry basket, too...

Friday

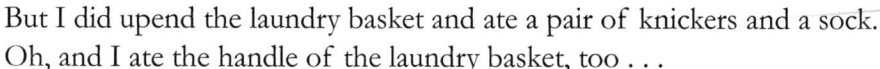

Interesting day. This morning, when my human was out, I ate all the Jibbitz off her Crocs. But that's all I did wrong, honest.

This afternoon she took us to work with her and I was petted and adored - obviously - by loads of people. Now we're back home and I'm in the garden practising my kangaroo jumps in the sun.

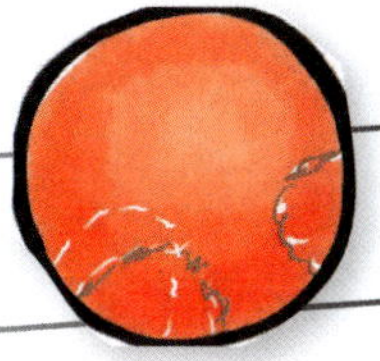

I might go upstairs in a bit and eat some of her clothes. Or the cat...

Saturday

My human is in a state of disbelief. She's not been well lately and needed a mega lie-in this morning so, before bed last night, she coated the downstairs with puppy pads and newspaper because I have a bit of a track record of 'accidents'.

When I clawed at her head to wake her up this morning after nearly 12 hours sleep, she discovered that there was no mess anywhere - I had been good all night (apart from nibbling the ear off one of her many, many, cuddly giraffes . . .).

See, I can do it if I want to, I just choose not to most of the time because it's more fun that way!

Saturday - Part 2

My human has been telling everybody today about how good I was last night and that maybe, just maybe, we've turned a metaphorical corner - hahahahahahahahaha!

When she was out at a meeting this evening, I wasted no time in reverting to type:

1. I did a poo on the landing.
2. I did two wees in the kitchen.
3. I am finally tall enough to reach right to the back corner of the kitchen counter so helped myself to the last 2 croissants and the only remaining tea cake. And I didn't share them with Calvie because he tried to stop me being naughty. I ignored him.
4. I pulled down the recycling bag, spilt out all the contents, chewed them all to bits and spread them around the house.

Ah, that's better!

5. I ate the strap off one of Emily's shoes.
6. I plucked a plastic cup out of the sink and chewed it, again, spreading the bits I didn't consume all over the house.
7. And finally, I nibbled a bit more of my favourite bookshelf in the bedroom.

Monday

Oh the indignity! My human now liberally plasters the house with 'puppy pads' when she goes out. Puppy pads, I ask you! I am seven and a half months old, practically a grown up dog and still she thinks I need such babyish things.

Well, to show my disgust, I tore them all to shreds and weed on Calvie's bed instead. That'll show her!

Wednesday

Amazing new discovery today; whilst nibbling the handles of the drawers at the bottom of my human's wardrobe, I found out, quite by accident, that if I nibbled at a particular angle, I could open the drawers! In the drawers were all sorts of nice, soft, chewy clothes which, not only did I chew and tear, but also I ran around the house with them in sheer delight, depositing them wherever I chose.

The wardrobe is one thing she can't move out of my ever-increasing reach - tee hee!

But what my human, nice though she is, doesn't seem to get is that what's hers is mine and what's mine I chew . . .

Thursday

Finally! I am long enough to reach to the back of the kitchen table where my human pushes everything against the wall to stop me from eating it - not anymore!

So, I nibbled her iPad case (couldn't open the case to eat the iPad though, unfortunately), pulled a table mat to pieces and scattered the pieces in an attractive post-modernist pattern around the kitchen, ate three pens, a plastic ruler, and a pencil.

What amused me the most was that, following the advice of some of you humans, she went out yesterday and bought two of those very expensive indestructible toys in which you hide doggy treats. I got my treats out within seconds of her leaving the house, stole Calvie's treats, and then set to work on the kitchen table.

A good day's work, methinks.

Saturday

To save me chewing things I shouldn't, my human gave Calvie and me an 'eternal bone' each when she went out this morning. I was as surprised as anybody to learn that eternity lasts only 12 minutes and 37 seconds, and that was for both bones . . .

All in all though, I did behave myself this morning but just now she popped out for 20 minutes or so . . .

Remember that new dog bed she bought recently? Well, I absolutely obliterated it and strewed the stuffing everywhere. And I do mean everywhere. It was even hilarious as she was cleaning it all up because it was a bit static and kept sticking to her clothes. She looked like Frosty the Snowman - hahahahahahahahaha!

Not that she found it funny, of course . . .
She gave me a massively stern lecture and I tried to look contrite - Calvie's been teaching me how - but I wasn't contrite at all (I thought it was just sooooooo funny!) so I don't think the look was very effective. Ho hum.

Monday

Phew! My human does still love me and is not going to send me back! I was still anxious when she went to work this morning so I did two poos and two wees in the kitchen. In hindsight, that probably wasn't the best response . . .

Anyway, my human doesn't want me to be anxious and she says she has tried everything to make me happy when she's out, which is true, but I just can't help fretting and this makes me do really bad things.

Next week we're going to see a lovely behavioural specialist at the vet where I was dumped all those months ago. I do like it there because they all treat me like a celebrity so hopefully there will be lots of people to make a fuss of me and lots of treats. And possibly some new furniture to chew!

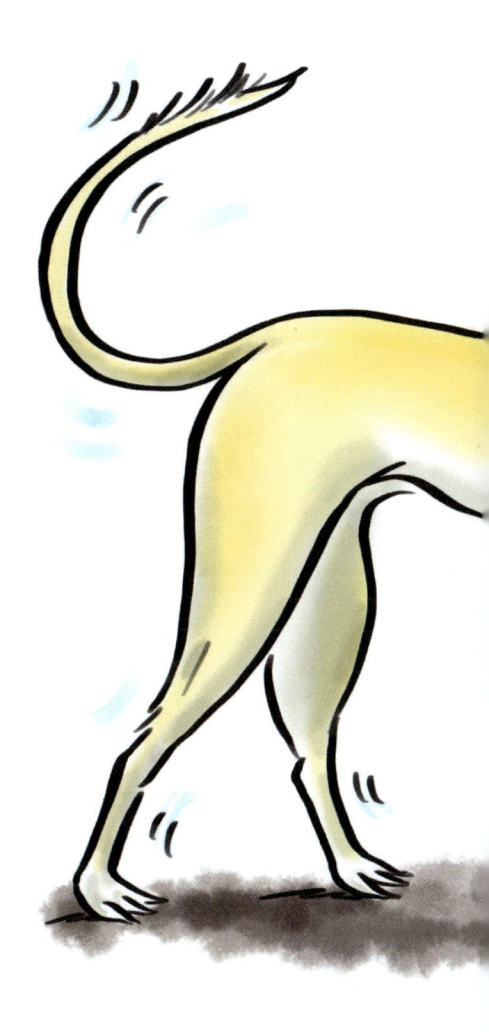

Wednesday

I have a Thundershirt! My human wrestled and wrestled to get it on me because I really didn't want to wear it but, once she succeeded, wow! It's amazing! My human was out most of today and I was calm and not stressed. I didn't chew anything I shouldn't, and I didn't wee or poo in the house.

You can imagine how devastatingly gorgeous I look in my bright red Thundershirt, can't you? (No need to answer that; it was rhetorical . . .) However (there has to be a 'however' where I'm concerned!), once she was home I stole her shoes and hid them and, when I was playing with Cal unsupervised in the garden, I ate a couple of plants and the rose off my human's watering-can.

Of course, my human is wondering if this good behaviour is just a one-off, a coincidence, or if the shirt really does work. I haven't decided yet . . .

Thundershirts are go!

Thursday

Well, I wish you could have seen and heard it! Yesterday evening when my human got home from work she let me and Calvie out to play in the garden. As it was such a lovely evening, she left the back door open for us to run in and out as we pleased whilst she got on with human stuff.

Cal and I had great fun wrestling and chasing round the garden and we also did several of our crazy, mad house-chases; we chase each other round the garden, in through the kitchen, through the hall, up the stairs, round the bedroom and back down again. All at top speed.

My human didn't notice that on one of these house-chases, I ran in with the manky plastic chicken toy that has been festering in the garden since some kind other human gave it to me for Christmas.

I buried said chicken in my human's bed and she only noticed it when she got into bed. Ha! She jumped a mile and squealed like a pig. I'm still laughing!

Friday

I have to be honest and tell you that, despite the Thundershirt, I have not been entirely good today.

I did manage to behave myself when my human was out at work this morning but then the famous Maestro Richard Howarth came round this afternoon. (Apparently he conducts some of the orchestras in which my human plays her vile-sounding French horn - such a noisy instrument; it puts me off my mischief-making when she practices.) I was so excited to meet him that I kept jumping up at him and trying to get him to wrestle with me. Apparently Maestro Richard isn't into wrestling - not with dogs anyway . . .

And then this evening when my human was out at orchestra I was a bit naughty again. There's just one bookcase left in her bedroom to which I have not done a great deal of damage so I decided to rectify that this evening . . .

Saturday

My human was out most of today for a rehearsal this afternoon and a concert this evening. Even though I was wearing my Thundershirt, I still didn't like it that she had left us so I tore apart the fold-up bed that her nephew uses when he comes to stay. It was under her bed and I've ignored it up until now but couldn't hold back any longer and it needed a lot of work so I needed plenty of time to destroy it, and today seemed like too good an opportunity to miss.

And when my human came home this evening, I was so very excited to see her that I ran and piddled on the kitchen floor, just to show her how much I had missed her. Oddly, she didn't seem to take it as a compliment . . .

Monday

Today, just to confuse my human, I have been very good when she's been out and a little devil when she's been at home!

When she got home from work, she got the hedge-trimmer out and attacked the ivy on the wall at the bottom of the garden. She got hot after a while

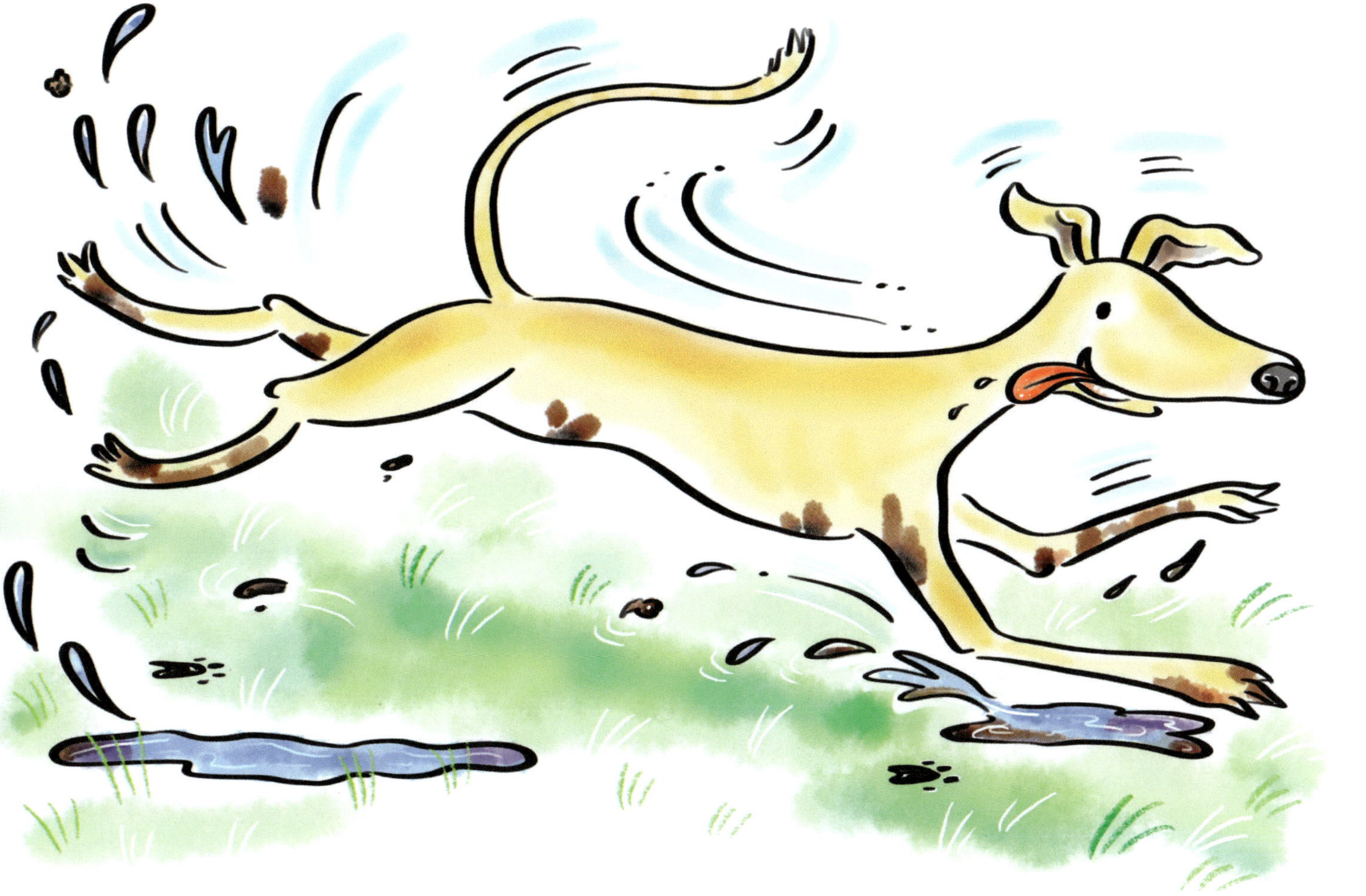

and took off her jumper, so I ate it. When she was clearing up all the cut-off bits of ivy, I pulled them out of the bin as quickly as she was putting them in and spread them all over the garden.

Then, whilst she was upstairs getting changed, I pulled down her plaster of Paris bandages again, bit open the packaging and spread the nasty white powder stuff all over the kitchen.

Finally, I managed to reach the new high-up place where she hides the recycling stuff and I pulled everything out and dragged it into the garden. That's all for now, but the night is still young...

Tuesday

Quite a productive day today. When my human was in work this morning I discovered that I'd had another growth spurt and was now able to reach into the pockets of her dressing gown hanging on the back of the bedroom door - my long, thin snout is perfect for this kind of stealthy work. I emptied out all the tissues from the pockets and made a wonderful design on the bedroom floor from the shredded bits.

This afternoon, a gloriously sunny afternoon, my human was working from home and stuck in front of her computer for hours - where's the fun in that?! Boring! So I made my own fun in the garden; I dug holes in the flower beds, pulled lots of plastic plant pots out of the greenhouse (which she'd opened to let in some air), did loads of kangaroo jumps with the flower pots stuck on the end of my nose, played tug-of-war with Calvie with some of the larger pots, then tore them into tiny pieces and scattered them around the garden.

Finally, when she was out at choir this evening I ate a hole in the seat of another pair of her trousers, and knocked over a glass of water on the kitchen table, thoroughly soaking a load of papers she had worked on this afternoon.

And now I'm rather tired so will go and curl up on her bed and refuse to move for the rest of the night . . .

Thursday

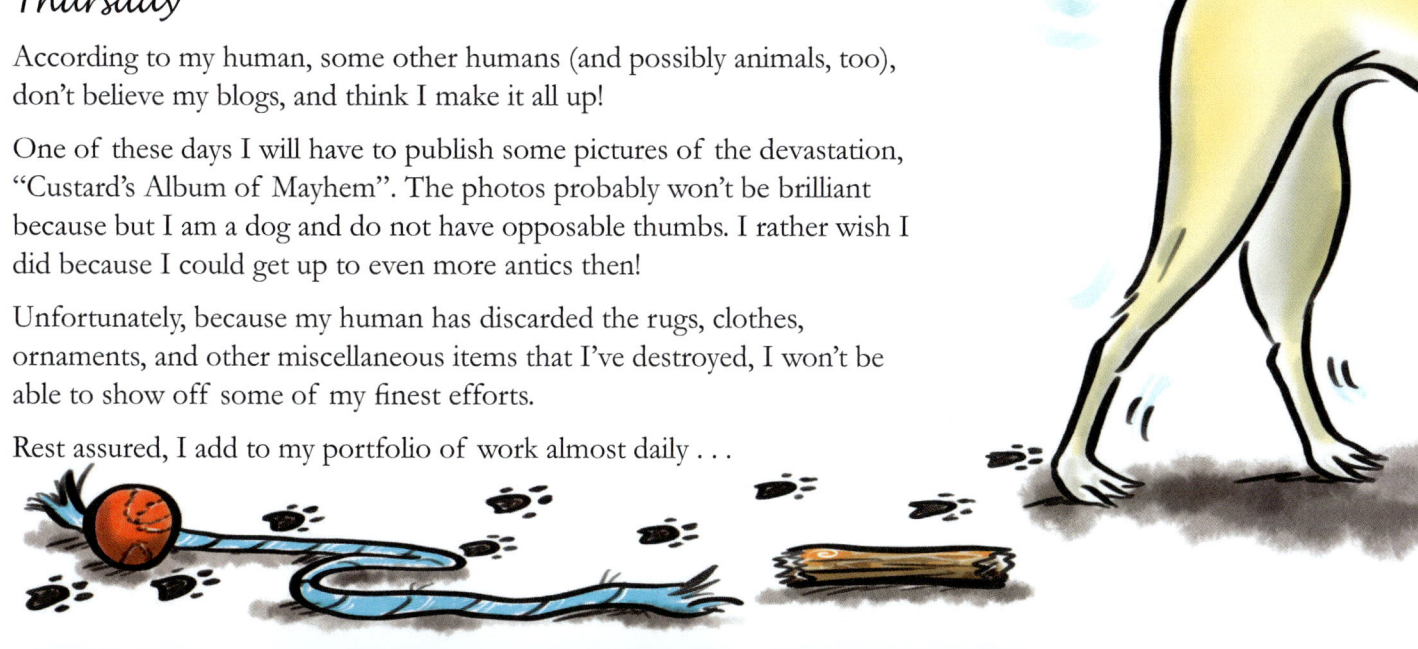

According to my human, some other humans (and possibly animals, too), don't believe my blogs, and think I make it all up!

One of these days I will have to publish some pictures of the devastation, "Custard's Album of Mayhem". The photos probably won't be brilliant because but I am a dog and do not have opposable thumbs. I rather wish I did because I could get up to even more antics then!

Unfortunately, because my human has discarded the rugs, clothes, ornaments, and other miscellaneous items that I've destroyed, I won't be able to show off some of my finest efforts.

Rest assured, I add to my portfolio of work almost daily . . .

Friday

I am so very excellent at this interior decorating malarkey that I'm thinking of making it my career.

My tips for that authentic 'gritty' feel in your home:

- Take one large, full bag of not-so-well-hidden cat litter (preferably Fuller's Earth).
- Tear open the bag.
- Drag the bag across the floor spilling the contents as you go.
- Let it fall naturally; you can always move bits around to create your own design later.
- Once you have emptied the entire bag, tear up the bag into little pieces and disperse among the cat litter.

You might add special touches of your own such as racing through the cat litter, spreading it further through the house, and leaving grey, gritty paw marks everywhere . . .

PS cushions look great outside on the lawn as well; don't be fooled into thinking that they should only be used indoors.

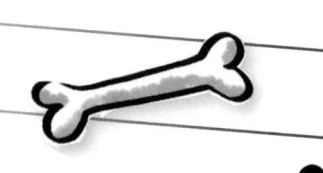

Monday

I've been really, really good for two whole days now! Although . . . my human has a bowl where she puts all the clutter from her coat pockets when she gets home; this bowl used to live on a low table by the front door. As I got taller she gradually moved the bowl further out of my reach and it now lives on a very high shelf above some coat pegs - you know the kind of thing. Anyway, she was late leaving the house this afternoon and forgot to put the bowl back on the high shelf when she'd taken out what she needed. What a gift! I ate three pencils, a pen, and her inhaler, and scattered a roll of poo bags all over the hall, tearing lots of them so she can't use them!

Ooh, the cat's just darted past to escape into the garden - must dash, byeeee!

Tuesday

Such drama last night! At about 1.30 am Calvie and I detected an alien presence in the house - someone or something that shouldn't be there. We barked our heads off and eventually woke my human who found we had cornered the intruder in the bathroom! It was a massive grey Tom cat who had come to invade Mimi-Cat's territory. Now, I'm no great friend of the evil Mimi (she has the sharpest claws in the world and constantly manages to escape when I try to eat her; it's most frustrating), but I am not going to allow an alien cat into my house; it's bad enough that one already lives here! Anyway, my human managed to get the intruder back outside but I was so wound up by the whole event that I wouldn't settle properly for ages so went downstairs and had a poo in the kitchen. I haven't done that for ages; it's great!

Oh, and when my human went out to work this morning, I ate a few more books, nibbled a couple more chunks out of the wardrobe and had a wee in the hall.

I didn't need to do any of these things but I have been really, really good for a couple of days and I do like to mix things up a bit, just to keep my human on her toes.

Sunday

I know I've not made a diary entry for a few days now, but I can assure you I have not been idle!

My human has been a bit under par of late so there's been lots of snuggling in her bed. Not because I feel sorry for her or anything, it's just that it's the warmest and most comfortable place to be . . .

And then my human's niece came to stay for a week. As she's just a pup herself, we played and played and played and were really quite naughty. (I've taught her not to take any notice of my human when we're called in for bed or to go off to school etc.)

Some other days I just did the usual stuff; eating books, drawer handles, shredding tissues, digging holes in the garden etc etc and yesterday, for no reason whatsoever, I piddled in the hall - just for the hell of it.

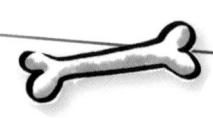

I've just stolen her French horn mouthpiece and hidden it in my bed. She probably knows where to look for it by now but I'm hoping she doesn't realise, before she starts to play, that I have covered it in dog slobber . . .

Monday

Rain, rain, rain, rain, rain! That's all there's been for days now. I hate the rain. My human keeps trying to take us out for walks but I just stand there shivering and looking pathetic until she relents and takes us home (Calvie loves going for a walk in any weather so I like to spoil it for him, too - ha!) So obviously, as I'm not expending my energy running around and practising my kangaroo jumps outside, I have to let off steam and go crazy inside. I like to thunder up and down the stairs for ages and pull all the bedding off my human's bed and abandon it halfway down the stairs so that I can try to catch that pesky cat who keeps tormenting me. Nasty thing scratched me on the face yesterday and as my skin is paper-thin, the scratch bled an awful lot. Luckily I bled all over my human's favourite rug so it wasn't all bad.

I was naughty today when my human was out as well. She keeps moving things out of my reach but I am now such a tall dog that there are few places left to which I cannot get. Today I reached right to the back of her desk and ate a birthday card and a house-warming card and present that she was about to post; a bit of the new book she has just started reading, and her all-important 'To do' list. And I emptied the paper recycling box. Not a bad morning's work on reflection.

Rain, Rain, Rain, I hate the rain!

Wednesday

Goals I have achieved since my last post:

- ☑ Terrorised cat
- ☑ Dug new holes in the lawn
- ☑ Nibbled pillow slips
- ☑ Removed drawer handles from chest of drawers
- ☑ Barked ferociously at hedgehog who visits the garden each night
- ☑ Random piddles in the kitchen
- ☑ Distributed plastic recycling around the house
- ☑ Hidden manky stick in human's bed
- ☑ Chewed human's shoes
- ☑ Stolen Calvie-dog's dinner
- ☑ Dug up plants in the garden
- ☑ Looked adorably cute after carrying out misdemeanours

Friday

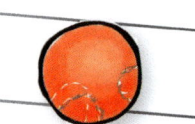

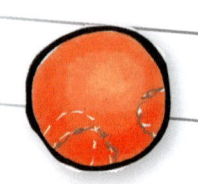

This is epic! Because I'm so narrow and so fast, I managed to escape through the garden gate when my human was bringing in the bins. I ran straight into the road but it was quiet and boring on our road so I sprinted on to the really busy main road at the end of our street. I had THE most brilliant time playing dodgem and slalom with all the cars, buses, lorries, and motorbikes but it made my human absolutely frantic. No idea why. Naturally all the vehicles stopped for me because I am so gorgeous and I was having such a fabulous time that I wouldn't go back to my human when she called, whistled, tempted me with treats etc. mainly because I wanted her and Calvie-dog to come and play in the road as well.

Miserable so-and-sos wouldn't play and eventually I got bored and went home. My human, instead of being impressed by my dodging skills and giving me lots of praise and treats, was really, really cross with me! Can you believe it?! It was almost as though she thought I'd done something stupid or dangerous . . .

Saturday

I hate rain and have refused to go out today but there was a brief respite so I had a mad moment in the garden racing around in huge circles for ages.

Sunday

There is absolutely no way to wear me out. After an eventful day of stealing and destroying things, and going for a huge, long walk, I roared around the garden again for hours this evening.

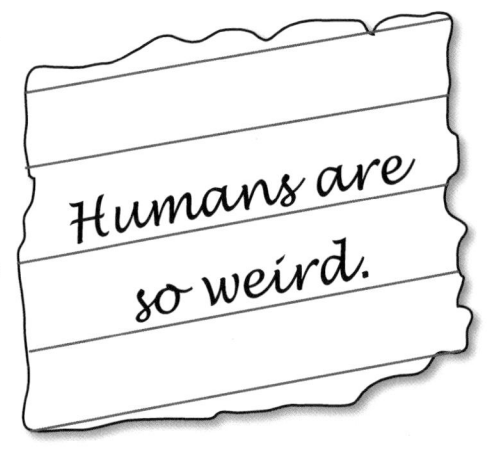

Humans are so weird.

Wednesday

I have mixed feelings about the vacuum cleaner; on the one hand, it's a scarily noisy machine that sucks up a lot of the mess I have taken a great effort to make but, on the other hand, it signifies that exciting visitors are imminent because that's the only time my human ever bothers with housework . . .

Tuesday

The last few days have been some of my naughtiest days ever! On Sunday evening my human took us for a great, long walk to wear me out. It was a lovely walk and I smelled lots of other dogs' bottoms, pooed in some nettles, chased some children, and even jumped in the lake, but then I realised my human was about to put me back on the lead and in the car - no way was I having that, so I ran off. I didn't go far, I ran around, always in sight, but just out of her reach. Half an hour later my human still hadn't caught me so she and Calvie got in the car and started to drive off without me! I ran after the car and she stopped to let me in but I ran off again - ha! My human drove off without me again! I suddenly realised I needed my dinner so deigned to get into the car when she stopped for a second time. She wasn't happy with me at all.

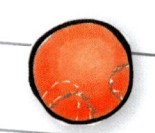

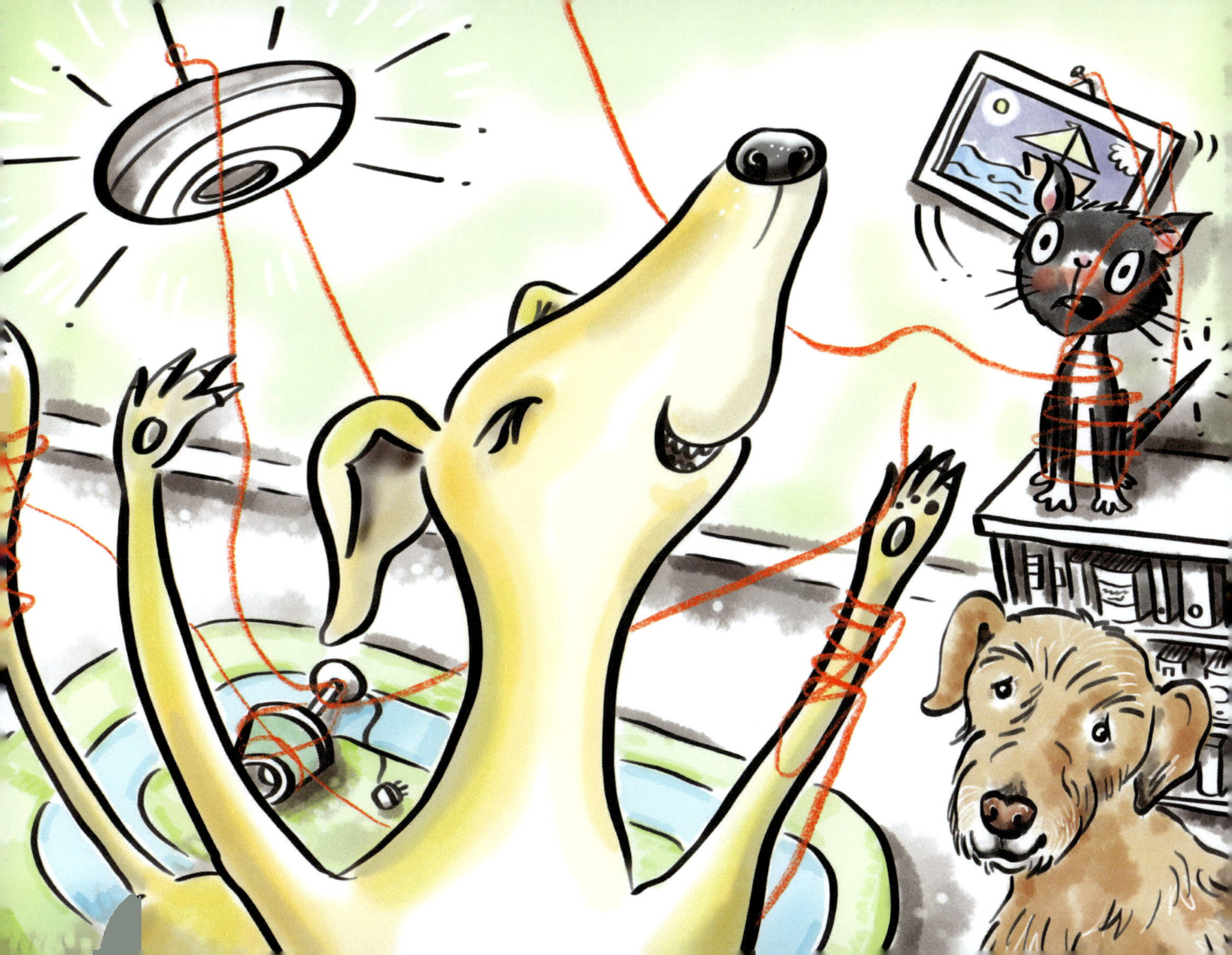

Then yesterday, I ate the entire telephone junction box where it comes into the house, as well as a good length of the telephone cable, and a bit of the window sill just for good measure - no messing about on the internet for my human; she should give all her attention to ME!

Today, a human man came to mend the telephone box and my human shut me in the kitchen because I kept trying to eat the human man's screwdriver and shoes. I didn't like being shut in the kitchen so I pulled the water pipes away from the wall and tore some wallpaper off the wall. And then I ate the temperature control thingy off the radiator and ran outside to dig some more holes in the lawn.

Why does my human get cross with me? Does anybody have any idea at all? I'm at a complete loss . . .

Wednesday

I stole a ball of wool - yay!!

Thursday

Yesterday, whilst my human was repairing some damage I had done in the house, I decided to wreak havoc in the garden. I dug two new, big holes in the lawn but, because I keep getting told off for that, I dug a mahoosive hole in one of the flower beds as well. Out of this hole I managed to dig up a lovely wisteria, roots and all, and a beautiful, well-established Jasmine plant. I spread soil, stones, roots and bits of vegetation all over the freshly-mown lawn.

Garden carnage is my new favourite thing - I love it!

Friday

I don't usually like rain but I've just discovered something wonderful about it; when it rains, all the holes I've dug in the lawn get water in the bottom and I can stick my long, long paws in them and make a lovely, muddy mess. And then I can run through the house, up the stairs, and trampoline on my human's bed - then I go back outside and do it all again. And again! Muddy paw prints everywhere - ha!

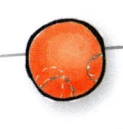

Saturday

Hahahahaha! My human was working on the computer yesterday evening and had left the back door open for Cal and me to run around outside as she worked. She was so engrossed that she didn't notice me slinking past her with a big stick from the garden. I ran upstairs and wriggled under her duvet where I happily chomped and shredded the stick for ages. Then I got bored so went back into the garden to dig more holes in the lawn, and completely forgot about the stick upstairs until my human went to bed! Oh my word, her reaction to finding tons of tiny bits of stick in her bed was priceless! Still laughing.

Monday

Double wowzers! My human has just taken us on the most epic holiday - there were miles and miles of mountainous sand dunes and long, long beaches to race around. I could be as hyperactive as I liked and chase the children sand-sledging in the dunes - even my human went sand-sledging. (Actually, to give her credit, it was her idea to do it - awesome idea, I love sand dunes!)

And, because all the humans lived in tents, I burrowed my way out at 5.30 every morning to go roaring round the campsite chasing rabbits and eating all the bits of food that the humans left lying around. Sneaking out at this time in the morning was wonderful because my human couldn't call and whistle me back in case she woke up everybody else, so I just got on with it and came back in my own good time, and my human had no idea where I went - ha! Can't wait to go camping again!

Wednesday

Well, I don't like this being back home lark; I want to go camping again. When we were camping my human was with us 24/7 and now we're home, she keeps leaving us to go to work or something, and I don't like it!

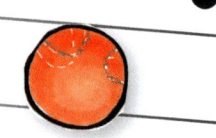

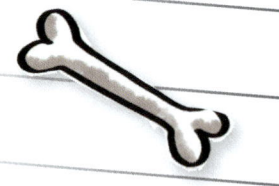

I've done a couple of protest poos, stolen a box of eggs and half a loaf, dug some more holes in the garden, and emptied the paper recycling box on a daily basis but it's not changed anything. I even hid a kitchen knife in her bed last night (after chewing the handle to bits) and shredded lots of sticks everywhere, but she still went out and left us again today. I'm going to have to put my really mischievous thinking-cap on to find a way to make her stay.

Sunday

There's soooooo much to tell you since I last had time to blog. My human had the audacity to go abroad on holiday and leave me and Calvie behind - can you credit it?! As it happens, we started off by staying with a lovely lady who looks after lots of dogs in her home when their owners are away so I had a fab time playing with all my new friends (after I'd piddled in her kitchen and eaten through the plastic clips on my harness so that it fell off and she couldn't catch me!).

But one day I was a bit too boisterous and had a nasty accident and cut my leg open. I cried and cried and cried and wanted my human but the kind lady took me to the vet who made me better. I cried at the vet's as well and got lots and lots of fuss off everybody, so it wasn't all bad.

The next day I was better again and played with all the other dogs as though nothing had happened.

And then, half-way through our stay, human Uncle Keith came and collected us and took us home with him to live with our best friends, Poppy and Bo, and he gave me a lovely new collar because I'd eaten my harness. I really like the new collar because it makes me look even more gorgeous than usual (difficult to imagine, I know . . .).

This evening was the best; we didn't know it was going to happen, but my human came and brought us home! I did actually miss her and was VERY excited to see her. So excited that I've just dug a great big hole in the garden and eaten one of her slippers.

Life is finally back to normal . . .

Monday

Hahahaha! It's hilarious watching the difficulty my human has mowing the lawn now that I've dug 26 holes in it!

Tuesday

Nobody really knows when I was born but the RSPCA adoption centre made an educated guess that it was on the 12th September last year. It's my 1st birthday today! Now I'm all grown up, perhaps it's time to refrain from naughtiness.

Nah!

Acknowledgements:

Many thanks to

my family and friends and to all at Team Author UK for helping me to publish this book about Custard.

To Sue Miller and Liat Ken-Dror for your design and publication support and Lisa Williams for brilliantly capturing Custard with your illustrations.

About the Author:

Jacqui Blore is a professional musician, story teller and crafter. She is best known for her work as The Story Teller and Piccolos Music, as well as being an integral part of the classical music scene throughout the North West.

As a story teller, Jacqui has worked for the National Trust, Sale Chamber Orchestra, Cambrian Orchestra, the Arts Council of Wales, Literature Wales, Llangollen International Musical Eisteddfod, Hereford Council, Wrexham County Borough Council, Pendine Park Care Home, and many schools and nurseries.

In 2016 Jacqui was commissioned by Sale Chamber Orchestra to write a book about their Children's Ambassador, "Minim Mouse". This led to the publication of her first book, "Minim Finds a French Horn", which was critically acclaimed and endorsed by the world's leading French Horn player, Sarah Willis. 2018 saw the publication of her second Minim book, "Minim Goes to The Proms".

Following the success of these two books, Jacqui began blogging about the escapades of her rescue pup, Custard.

The "Dogblog" posts soon gained a huge following on social media and followers begged for a book of Custard's diary – this is the result.

www.piccolosmusic.org

info.piccolosmusic@gmail.com

@Piccolos Music and The Story Teller

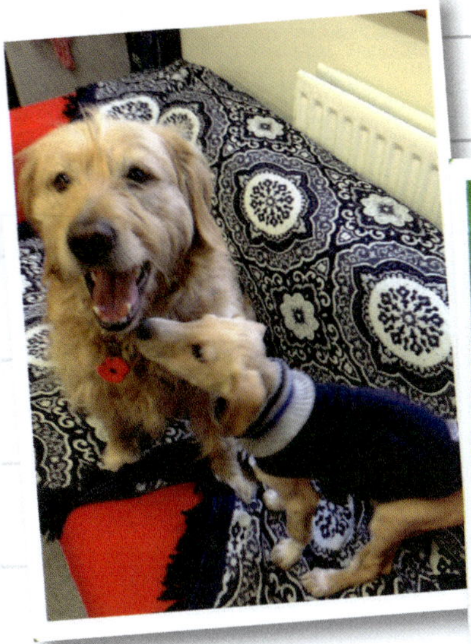
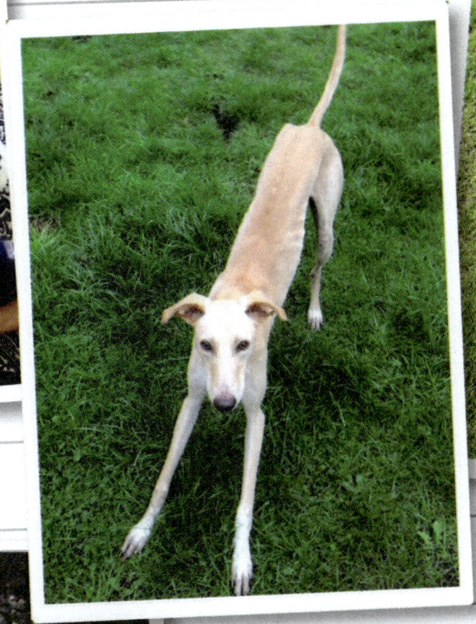
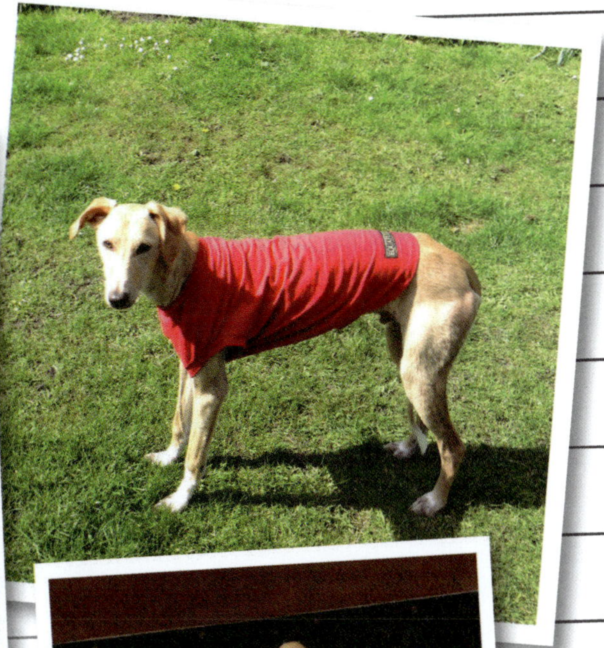
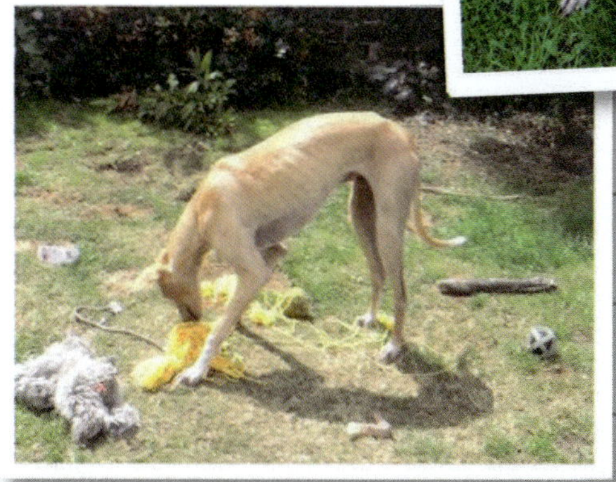
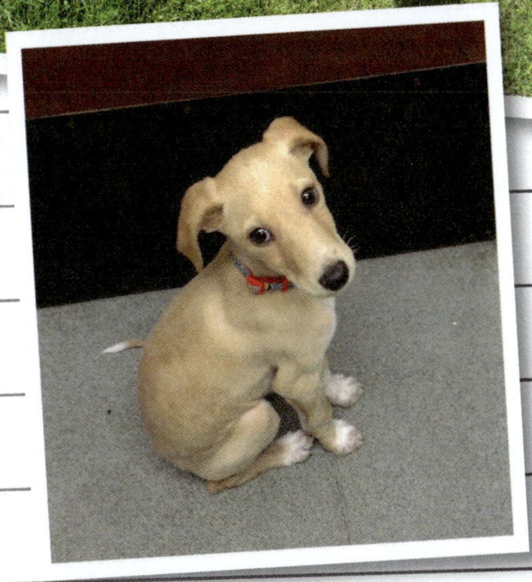

32808654R00033

Printed in Poland
by Amazon Fulfillment
Poland Sp. z o.o., Wrocław